Mikey's Place

Written and illustrated by
Steve Giddings

Go to www.stevesmusicroom.com/mikeys-place for free teaching materials and extras!

Text and illustrations copyright © 2023 Steve Giddings

All rights reserved. This publication is protected by copyright, and permission should be obtained from the publisher prior to a prohibited reproduction, storage in a retrieval system, or transmission in any form or by any means, electronic, mechanical, photocopying, recording, or likewise. For information regarding permission, write to steve@stevesmusicroom.com.

ISBN (flipbook) 978-0-9959155-6-5
ISBN (paperback) 978-0-9959155-3-4
ISBN (French paperback) 978-0-9959155-4-1

Steve's Music Room Publishing (Kids Division)
Prince Edward Island
Canada
www.stevesmusicroom.com

Mikey sang in the bath.

He sang during math.
It was something that he loved to do.

Mikey's song, it turned sad,
it was really too bad.
He couldn't find where he fit in!

He needed a place.
Mikey wanted his space.
But he didn't know where to begin.

He just couldn't stand
the old microphone band.
They gave too much awful feedback.

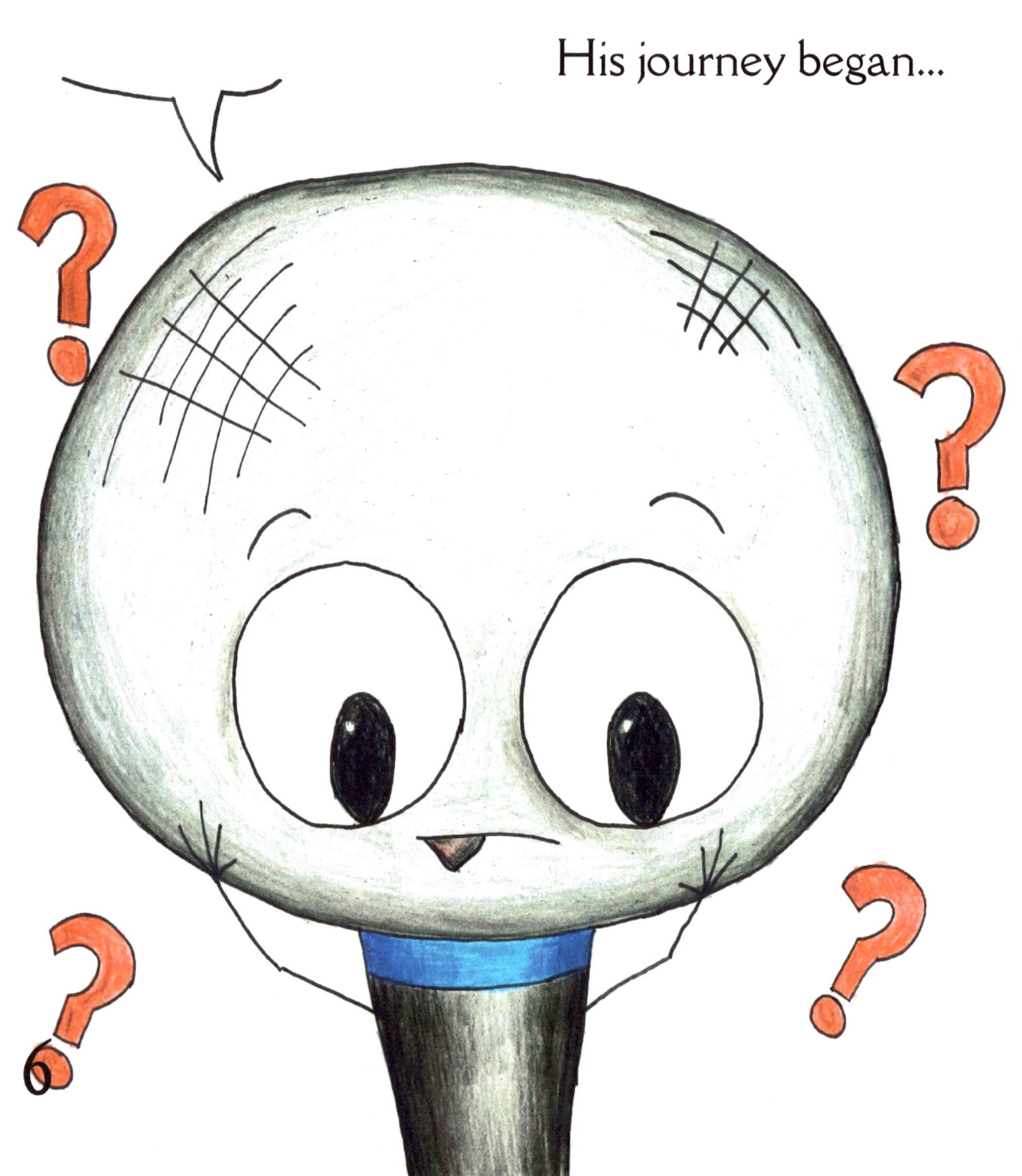

...with a stroll.

But he didn't expect
where the dots would connect.
The mic soon would discover his role.

He hadn't gone far,
when he met a...

...guitar

who seemed to be holding it down.
"I have six plucky things...

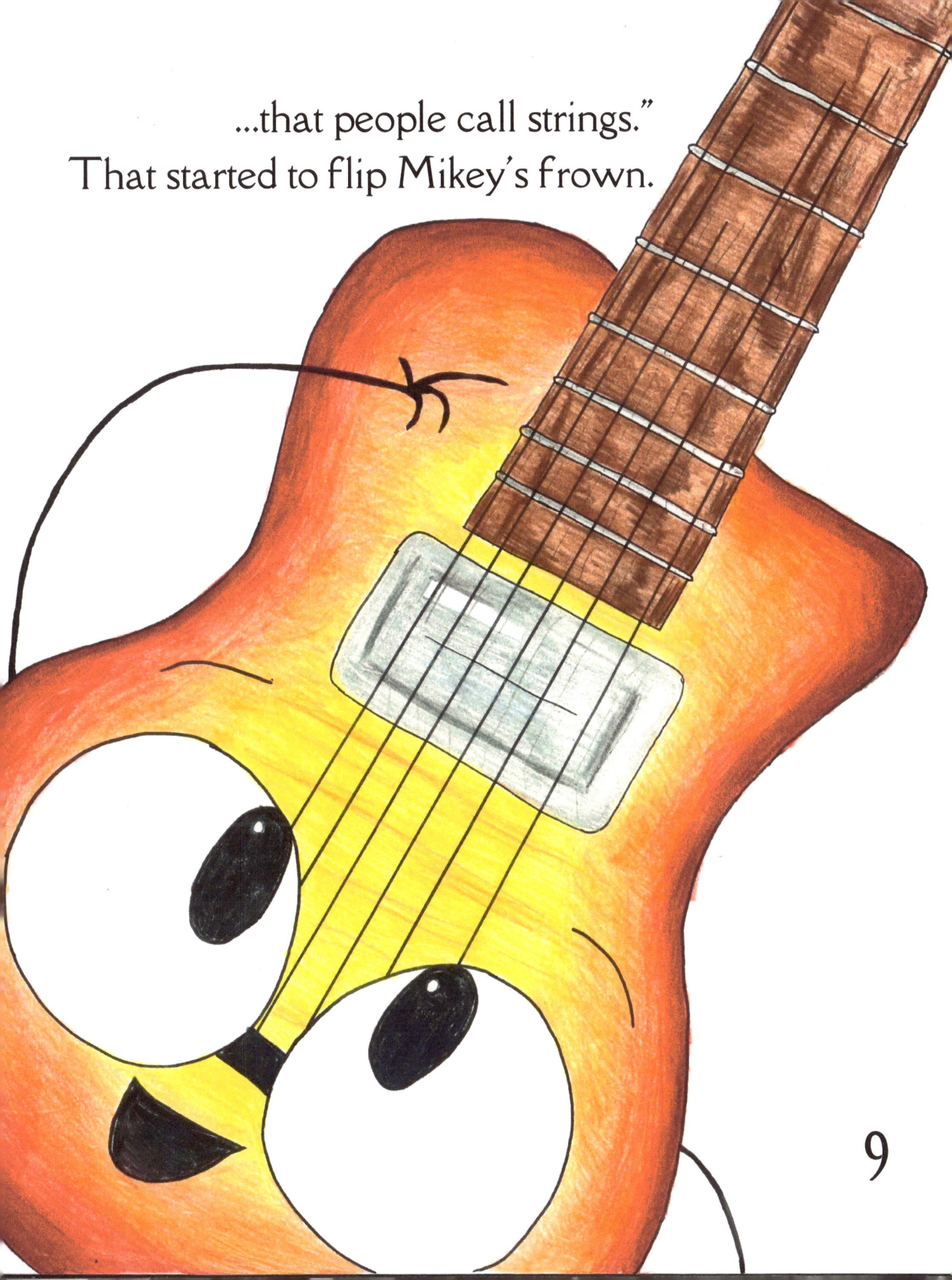
"...that people call strings."
That started to flip Mikey's frown.

And they got along
as if in the same song,
so the microphone told him his bind.

"My band's a quartet.
They'll like you, I bet!"
So the microphone followed behind.

They got to the spot,
Mikey loved it, and thought,
"Could this be the place I am needed?"

This place, it felt warm.
Was it Mikey's platform?
Mikey's puzzle would soon be completed.

...a **drum kit** rolled onto the floor!

"We use sticks on my head."

"Right here!" the kit said.

"I help the band count up to four."

A **bass** with thick strings arrived to play things, to bolster the band's harmonies.

"I'm a **keyboard**," she said,
coming in from the shed,
"I can play all the backgrounds or leads."

"I have black and white keys...

...and you press them in threes.

I can play any sound the band needs."

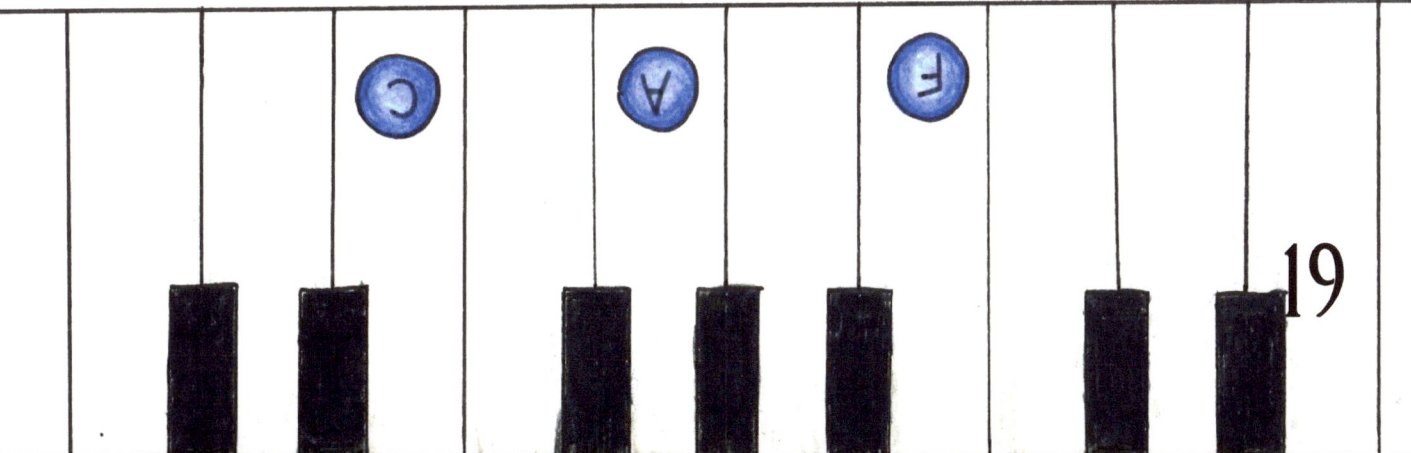

"We need someone on vox;
there's no one here but this fox.

Perhaps you could join us today?"

Mike was nervous at first.
He was so unrehearsed!
But then the group started to play.

Mikey's home—it was found!
It turned him around.
It gave him the means to create.

The friends gave a hand
as they formed their rock band,
and their sounds were considered top rate.

And their audience grew
when they made their debut.
They put on their finest showcase.

www.ingramcontent.com/pod-product-compliance
Lightning Source LLC
Chambersburg PA
CBHW041542040426
42446CB00002B/204